...per

The Empire State
Building in New York City

Prestel

What's the most famous skyscraper in the world?

Most people think it's the Empire State Building in New York City. With 102 floors and a height of 1,250 feet, it surely was the world's tallest structure for many years. Built in a record time of only eighteen months, people called it the Eighth Wonder of the World. In 1933 a Hollywood movie immortalized the building when King Kong scaled its heights holding a terrified woman under his arm. And although there are now numerous buildings that are even taller, this one has remained a symbol for New York and America, and for courage and adventure.

The Empire State Building was constructed between 1929 and 1931. At times there were 3,500 people – the population of a small town! – working on the site. One of them was Joe Carbonelli, just sixteen years old. His job was to carry drinking water up to the workers.

This blow-up King Kong climbed the Empire State in 1983!

As a young boy

Joe used to climb onto the roof of his apartment building in Brooklyn. From there he could see the Manhattan skyline with its many tall buildings clustered together like lofty mountain peaks, sparkling against the evening sky.

Joe liked the Woolworth Building best. It was the tallest building in the world, and its tower made it look like a stretched out church. Built in 1913, it was exactly as old as he was.

HIGHEST BUILDING IN THE WORLD, 750 FEET ABOVE THE SIDEWALK, 57 STORIES.

FLOOR AREA 27 ACRES, 34 ELEVATORS.   APPROXIMATE COST $13,500,000

70908 WOOLWORTH BUILDING, NEW YORK   COPR. DETROIT PUBLISHING CO.

Equitable Building, New York.

Singer Building, New York.

Woolworth Building and Broadway, New York.

Times Building, N.Y. City. 5. 6. 11.

WILSON

METROPOLITAN LIFE BUILDING, NEW YORK
HEIGHT 680 FEET, 48 STORIES
HIGHEST BUILDING IN THE WORLD.

Flat Iron Building, New York.

rk Row Building, New-York.

CHRYSLER BUILDING, NEW YORK CITY   II

Bank of the Manhattan Co.
Wall Street
New York City

Joe collected picture postcards

of New York skyscrapers. Almost like looking at the players
on baseball cards, here Joe could track how the magnificent
towers had changed in the past few decades. They were not
only much taller now, but they also looked different. They
were no longer allowed to rise straight up from the street; now
the buildings soared upwards in a series of steps. This way
more light fell on the street and on the neighboring buildings.

Recently the newspapers had reported that a new skyscraper
planned for either New York or Chicago would surpass the
record height of the Woolworth Building. Joe was excited.
"Will it be in New York?" he wondered. Then he heard about a
new bank on Wall Street that had just topped the Woolworth
Building and was still growing. At the same time, further
north, the Chrysler Building was going up. "Which building
will be the tallest?" Joe wondered. Suddenly, at the very last
minute, the architect of the Chrysler Building, William Van
Alen, raised an antenna on its top. It was a new world record!
But by then the plans for the Empire State Building were also
on the drawing board. . .

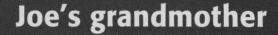

Joe's grandmother

couldn't understand why he loved tall buildings. "Only sinners build skyscrapers," she said again and again. "Do you remember the story about the Tower of Babel? It brought only unhappiness. New York is the new Babylon – it's not right to try to reach Heaven with our buildings! Nothing should be higher than the church spires!"

Perhaps Joe's grandmother was right. While the two skyscrapers in New York were racing neck in neck to break the height record, the Great Depression set in. Suddenly countless companies went bankrupt, and the employees landed on the streets – without jobs. It was hard to believe what the

The Tower of Babel is a famous tall building described in the Bible.

newspaper was announcing: the construction of a new, even taller structure, and hundreds of new jobs for construction workers.

Joe had just turned sixteen and it was time he found a job. He could hardly believe how lucky he was to find work with Starrett and Eken Brothers, the construction company that was building the giant new tower. He was taken on as a water boy, and it was his job to make sure that all the workers had enough to drink. He earned five dollars a week.

Trinity Church and Skyscrapers at Night, New York.

19623

Joe's first day at work

was September 24, 1929. When he got to Fifth Avenue, he saw the long line of 600 workers standing in front of the old Waldorf Astoria Hotel, ready to start. Joe had no idea that the team of construction workers would grow to six times that number, and that there would be twenty water boys instead of five.

Joe received a metal ID tag with his name on it, a metal bucket, and three glasses. All day long he marched back and forth and up and down, carrying water to the workers. It was important not to miss a single workman who might complain to the foreman of being thirsty.

First of all, the workers had to tear down the Waldorf Astoria Hotel, which stood where the new skyscraper was going to go up. It was an old-fashioned hotel, and Joe had never seen rooms as grand as the ballroom or the Palm Garden. It took more than eighty days to take the hotel apart, a process that was fascinating for Joe to watch. First the workers put up the scaffolding. This allowed them to work safely, and helped to protect pedestrians from falling stones. The hotel had been built around a steel frame, just like the future Empire State Building would be. To take it down, the workers had to cut up the heavy steel *girders* with welding torches and lower each girder to the ground with a crane. Finally, they smashed the walls with wrecking balls or blew them up with dynamite. By the beginning of February there was nothing left of the hotel. Then the workers began to drive *piles* into the ground for the foundation of the new building. They had to be deep enough for the weight of the huge structure to rest on the solid *bedrock*.

THE WALDORF-ASTORIA, NEW YORK
GRAND BALL ROOM, ARRANGED FOR PRIVATE THEATRICALS

THE WALDORF-ASTORIA, NEW YORK, GRILL ROOM (SUPPER DANCE)

THE WALDORF-ASTORIA, NEW YORK, MAIN FOYER (EVENING CONCERT)

10

girder: a horizontal beam that supports weight above it – like the floors of a skyscraper.

pile: a long, slender column made of steel, timber, or reinforced concrete driven into the ground to carry weight above it.

bedrock: the solid rock that lies deep beneath the soil.

On April 1, 1930,

the first large steel supports arrived. Manufactured in Pittsburgh, they were transported to New York by train, ship, and large trucks. The workers inserted 210 of them into the concrete foundations, and from then on the building rose rapidly. Some days the building grew by an entire floor. In May, when Joe crossed the Brooklyn Bridge in the morning, he could see the large steel structure poking its head above its neighbors. By August he was carrying water up to the steel workers on the fiftieth floor. It was now as high as the Woolworth Building, but still only half as high as planned! In September the steel frame was eighty-five floors high – only the large mast and the antenna were missing. On some days the view Joe could see was breathtaking. Around him was the metropolis of Manhattan, and in the east was Brooklyn where he lived.

Joe liked to spend time with the workers who fixed the large steel girders together with *rivets*. They worked in teams of four. One man heated the steel rivets in a coal oven until they were glowing hot. Then he threw one of the rivets to another worker who caught it in a large metal funnel, picked it up with a pair of tongs, and placed it in one of the pre-drilled holes in the steel girder. The rivet was then pressed firmly from both sides with a *pneumatic hammer*. During the cooling process the rivet contracted, pulling the steel girders together. The workers used approximately 100,000 rivets to build the Empire State Building.

rivet: a pin or bolt with a head like a nail, used for joining two pieces of metal. The pin is driven through a hole in both pieces of metal and then hammered down at the other end to fasten it.

pneumatic hammer: a special tool that uses air pressure to fire rivets into girders.

But Joe didn't have much time to watch. The work was dusty and the workers were thirsty. "This water isn't fresh; it doesn't taste good!" complained Vladimir Korloff, the brawny Russian man on the demolition team. The next day Joe brought lemons and some salt from home. The water tasted better, and Joe got more tips. In some weeks he made more in tips than in his standard wages.

The structure grew and grew. The next step was to fill out the large, empty steel skeleton. Bricklayers, carpenters, and concrete workers came to make the ceilings. Stonemasons put up the limestone facing, and metal workers installed the decorated aluminum plates on top of the limestone. There were also electricians, plumbers, and many other workmen who did their specialized jobs. Joe met many of them on his rounds, and some of them became his friends.

In order to transport the building material rapidly, rails were laid on some of the floors so that the workers could easily push the carts of materials back and forth.

Soon there were some water pipes on the upper floors, and Joe was able to concentrate on taking water to the top floors. How proud he was to be able to go up in the large freight elevators! On other construction sites the workers were carried up in cranes, which was much more dangerous.

From time to time the foreman would say, with a serious expression on his face: "Today the governor is coming. I don't want to see anyone standing around and not working. After all, the governor is paying for all of this."

The "governor" was a man called Al Smith, who had actually been governor of the state of New York until he had decided to run for the presidency and lost. Now he was interested in constructing the tallest building in the world. He drummed up financial support and kept the press well informed. His partner, John Raskob, was a financial genius who for many years had managed the finances of General Motors, the largest American automobile company. In the middle of the Great Depression the two of them had succeeded in making this huge project happen. Everything turned out to be much cheaper – especially labor and steel – because of the depression. As a result, the building cost only half of what they had originally calculated. Joe saw Mr. Smith and Mr. Raskob only once from far away. They were constantly surrounded by men dressed in expensive-looking suits.

Every once in a while the architect, William Lamb,

visited the construction site. Joe admired him more than any of the other well-dressed visitors. He very much wanted to meet him, just once. One day, when Joe came by with his bucket of water and saw Mr. Lamb looking over the plans with a foreman, he gathered up all his courage. "Would you like something to drink, Sir?" he asked. "Well, why not? Thank you, my boy," Mr. Lamb replied. When the architect noticed that Joe was interested in the plans, he rolled out a drawing and said, "Look at this. Here's the ground floor, and this is the thirtieth floor. Toward the top the building gets smaller, but you know that, don't you? And at the top it's pointed like a huge pencil." Joe looked at the large blue plans, called "blueprints," that smelled of ammonia. "For everything we do, there is some kind of sign or symbol in the ground plan," the architect explained. "This is the outer wall, here are the windows. These crosses in the middle are the shafts for the fifty-eight elevators. And now I have to get back to work. So long, water boy, and thanks again!"

Plan of the 74th to 78th floors

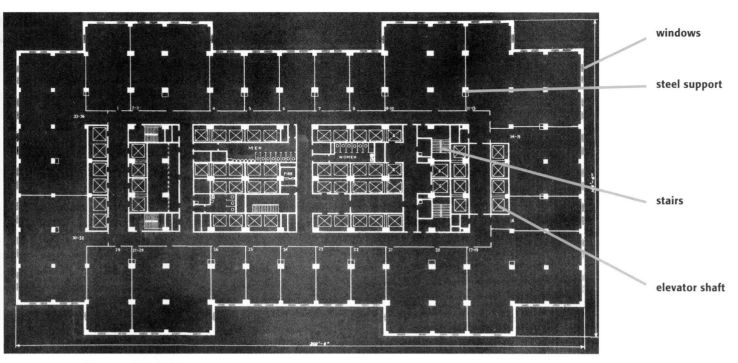

windows

steel support

stairs

elevator shaft

Plan of the 6th to 20th floors

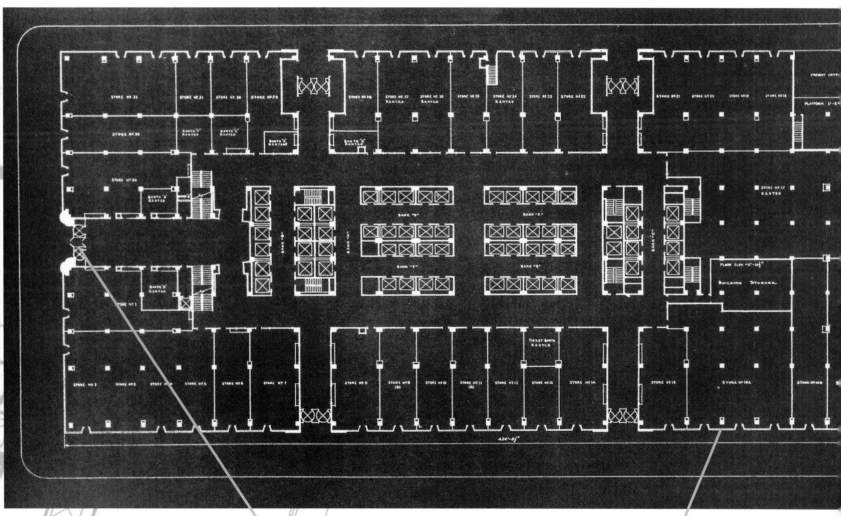

Ground floor

revolving door

window at street level

19

"That crazy photographer is at it again,"

Lewis Hine, 1935

said the foreman when he saw a man with a camera at the site. It was actually "Governor" Al Smith who had asked Lewis Hine, the famous photographer, to record all the details of the Empire State Building's construction.

Lewis Hine was particularly interested in the workers. For him they were the true heroes, the people who risked their lives for the building. He loved to take dramatic photos: sometimes he would ask the workers to climb over the side of the building on a rope or to stand on the iron ball at the end of the crane's cable. When the security officer saw these antics, he was horrified. The workers were instructed to work cautiously, and, of course, it was forbidden to hang over the edge of the steel frame just for fun. Besides, when Hine was taking his photos, it distracted the other workers. But to this day these photos are the most impressive pictures of a high-rise construction site. Of course, Lewis Hine also took photos of the security officer, a serious man in his late thirties who climbed up into the most remote corners to see that every rivet was tight and the construction solid. He also made sure that there were no oil spots on the girders for other workers to slip on. When it rained, work had to stop – at least on the top floors where the workers were exposed to the weather.

One day, when Joe stopped for a moment to watch Lewis Hine at work, the photographer suddenly turned around and said: "Boy, how old are you? Children shouldn't be working." When Joe explained proudly that he was sixteen years old and a grown-up, Hine replied, "Well, I guess that's OK. You're only a year younger than my son Corydon, and he helps me a lot." Corydon often came to the site and helped his father set up the heavy camera and change the lens. One time Joe asked when he could see the photos. "They'll all appear in a book made for young people like you and Corydon. But I haven't thought of a title yet." "How about *Men at Work*?" Joe asked.★

★ Lewis Hine's book *Men at Work* appeared in 1932 and was awarded a prize for young people's books.

There were many Native Americans – Mohawks from Canada – among the steel workers.

When they were talking to each other in their native language, Joe couldn't understand a word. They spoke English, too, in an unusual, singsong way. They weren't afraid of heights – they walked around the steel girders on the fortieth floor as though they were taking a walk in Central Park. Joe wasn't so lucky, and he felt dizzy when he was up so high. The Mohawks taught him what to do. "Don't ever look down; look straight ahead at the end of the girder; never look down." One time Joe slipped on a little drop of oil. As he fell, he was able to catch hold of a girder in the last second. He was shaking all over when the Mohawks brought him to safety. After he had come to his senses again, he went down to his boss on the ground floor. "I'm not going up there again today." "Then you're fired," was the reply. The foreman knew that this was the only way for Joe to overcome his fear. Later on in life Joe often recalled what he had learned from this experience: be cautious, but don't give up too soon!

Not everyone was so fortunate. There was one icy winter day that Joe would never forget. It was January 31, the day Giuseppe Tedeschi and Luis DeDominichi slipped and fell. Joe had known both of them. All in all, six workers lost their lives while working on the Empire State Building.

25

For Joe, everything went much too quickly.

In April the building was finished, much earlier than expected. On May 1, 1931, there was a big opening day party, to which all the workers were invited. On the following day the newspapers reported that Al Smith had been there with his children and had cut the red ribbon.

When Joe entered the building, he hardly recognized it. Everything was covered with marble. Metal plaques hung on the walls listing the most important roles of the construction workers: such as metal workers, elevator specialists, and electricians. Joe searched in vain for the water boys. He found one plaque which honored many of his friends for their exceptional work: Matthew McKean, who had built the wooden forms for the reinforced steel ceilings; Charlie Sexton, the merry mason; and Thomas Walsh, the thirsty crane operator. Today visitors can still read these names in the entry hall.

The elegant metal tower at the top of the building was built as a mooring mast for dirigibles – an early type of airship that could be steered. The mooring mast was tested twice in September 1931, but it was simply too windy at the top of the Empire State for the airships to dock. Using a telescope, Joe watched the maneuver from the roof of his house in Brooklyn. He didn't really mind that the airships could not dock. Instead, another visitors' observatory was erected on the 102nd floor, and later an antenna mast was placed on top of the observatory.

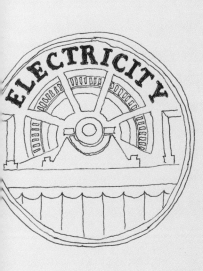

Several years passed, and Joe was grown with two sons of his own, and working as a mason on another construction site when there was a terrible accident. A U.S. bomber whose pilot was lost in heavy fog crashed into the sixtieth floor of the Empire State Building. The pilot and several people in the building and on the street below could not be saved – it was a terrible day for the Empire State.

In 1974, when the Sears Tower in Chicago became the tallest building in the world, Joe was getting ready to retire. That's how long it took to break the old height record. Most New Yorkers were disappointed. Joe, however, was still proud of "his" skyscraper and continued, even as an old man, to take friends, visitors, and his grandchildren to the Empire State Building and to tell them about his experiences as a water boy. And from time to time he climbed onto the flat roof of his house in Brooklyn to look at Manhattan, with the Empire State Building gleaming in the sun.

Joe Carbonelli and many others mentioned in this book were actually employed in the construction of the Empire State building. Joe lived to a ripe old age, and passed away only recently in New York City.

Eiffel Tower, Paris 1,050 ft (32(

Empire State Building, New York City 1,250 ft (381 m)

The Pyramids at Giza, Egypt 482 ft (147 m)

Ulm Cathedral, Germany 532 ft (162 m)

Big Ben, London 315 ft (96 m)